MOUNT RAINIER NATIONAL PARK

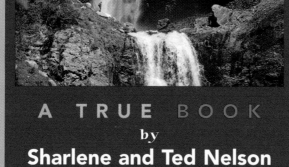

A TRUE BOOK

by

Sharlene and Ted Nelson

Children's Press®
A Division of Grolier Publishing

New York London Hong Kong Sydney
Danbury, Connecticut

Indian paintbrush

Reading Consultant
Linda Cornwell
Learning Resource Consultant
Indiana Department
of Education

Subject Consultant
Loren E. Lane
Resource Education Specialist
Mount Rainier National Park

Technical Review
Steven Brantley
U.S. Geological Survey

Visit Children's Press on the Internet at:
http://publishing.grolier.com

Library of Congress Cataloging-in-Publication Data

Nelson, Sharlene P.
    Mount Rainier National Park / by Sharlene and Ted Nelson.
    p.   cm. — (A true book)
    Summary: Describes the history, landscape, wildlife, and activities for
visitors at Washington's Mount Rainier National Park.
    ISBN: 0-516-20624-9 (lib. bdg.)   0-516-26381-1 (pbk.)
    1. Mount Rainier National Park (Wash.)—Juvenile literature. [1. Mount
Rainier National Park (Wash.) 2. National parks and reserves.] I. Nelson,
Ted W. II. Title. III. Series.
F897.R2N45 1998
979.7`782—dc21   97-8233
                                                                      CIP
                                                                      AC

Contents

Pacific
Northwest

0   200 miles

0   300 kilometers

N
W   E
S

WASHINGTON

● Seattle

● Tacoma

● Spokane

★ Olympia

Mt. Rainier
National Park

IDAHO

Columbia River

OREGON

PACIFIC OCEAN

Sunrise
Visitor Center ○

▲ **Mt. Rainier**

Henry M.
Jackson
Visitor
Center

Grove
of the
Patriarchs ○

○ Paradise

Ohanapecosh
River

○ Longmire

A Mountain Park

Mount Rainier stands 14,411 feet (4,392 meters) high. It is the highest mountain in the area of the United States called the Pacific Northwest. The mountain is so big that it can be seen from 100 miles (160 kilometers) away.

From the mountain's top, rock and ice give way to

Mount Rainier is the highest mountain in the Pacific Northwest.

meadows covered by summer-time flowers. Farther down the mountain, there are thick forests of evergreen trees.

The mountain, its meadows, and forests are in Mount Rainier National Park in Washington State. The park covers 235,612 acres (95,389 hectares).

There are forests, meadows, and lakes in Mount Rainier National Park.

Fire and Ice

Mount Rainier is a sleeping volcano. It has not erupted in many years. More than 500,000 years ago, lava (melted rock) erupted from an opening called a vent in the earth's crust. As the lava cooled, it turned to rock.

Over time, there were thousands more eruptions. Sometimes the lava exploded into the

Mountain streams flow over volcanic rocks formed by long-ago eruptions.

air. Clouds of ash and gas rose high into the sky. At other times, the lava flowed down the volcano's sides. There was so much lava turning into rock that the mountain kept growing higher.

9

During the time of these eruptions, the earth's climate was sometimes warm. At other times, it was very cold. The cold times were known as the ice ages. Snow fell and formed great masses of ice. These masses are called glaciers.

During the ice ages, glaciers covered the mountain and the valleys below it. The glaciers moved slowly down the mountain like rivers of ice. They carved rocks from the volcano's

During the ice ages, glaciers like this covered the entire mountain.

sides. About twelve thousand years ago, the climate began to warm again. Most of the glaciers melted.

About five thousand years ago, a landslide destroyed the top of Mount Rainier. Rocks mixed with melted snow and ice plunged down the mountain into the valleys far below.

Today, the earth's climate is warmer. But large amounts of snow still fall in the park every year. The most snow Mount Rainier National Park ever had was during the winter of 1971–72. About 93 feet (28 m) of snow fell! Some of the

Glaciers still cover the mountain's top (above). In winter, some of the park's buildings are covered with snow (right).

snow that falls in the park freezes into ice. There are twenty-five glaciers on Mount Rainier's highest slopes. These glaciers continue to carve and shape the mountain.

Steam from vents at this crater's rim keeps the rocks free of snow and ice.

Near the mountain's top, steam and hot gases rise from vents. The steam is a constant reminder that helps scientists to know that Mount Rainier could erupt again.

The First People

For centuries, Yakima, Nisqually, and Puyallup American Indians lived in the lowlands around the mountain. They hunted deer and bear in the forests. They picked berries in the meadows. They caught fish in rivers that flowed down the mountain. The Indians had

different names for the mountain. Some called it Ta-co-bet, or "the place where the water comes from." Others called it Takhoma, or "great white mountain."

The name Mount Rainier was given to the mountain in 1792 by the English explorer, Captain George Vancouver. He named it for an English admiral, Peter Rainier.

Captain George Vancouver

James Longmire settled near Mount Rainier in 1853. Long-mire became friends with the Indians and learned where their trails were. In 1870, he helped one of the first groups of white people to reach the mountain's summit.

Longmire also discovered warm, bubbling springs where he built a small hotel. A spring is a place where water rises up from underground. To serve his guests cold drinks, Longmire chopped ice from a nearby

James Longmire (left) built the first hotel (above) in what would later become a national park.

glacier. His springs and hotel later became part of the park.

In 1888, Longmire helped other visitors to climb the mountain. One of them was the naturalist, John Muir. Muir

John Muir

decided that the mountain should be a national park. After years of political debate, President William McKinley dedicated Mount Rainier National Park in 1899.

John Muir

John Muir was born in Scotland in 1838. He came to the United States in 1849. Muir traveled throughout the country and wrote about the plants and animals he saw. His writings helped people to appreciate nature.

John Muir worked to have areas of land saved forever as national parks. His efforts helped to preserve lands in California, Alaska, and Washington.

Muir died in 1914. In his honor, sites in several parks have been named after him.

Climbers to the Top

By the time Mount Rainier became a park, one hundred people and one dog had climbed the mountain. Many climbers carried long walking sticks. Some climbers screwed spikes into their boots to keep from slipping on the ice. They climbed

Climbers make their way to the top of Mount Rainier.

over glaciers and up steep ice walls.

Today, about ten thousand people climb Mount Rainier each summer. Guides lead them up trails marked in the ice. The climbers carry ice axes and wear steel spikes strapped to their boots. On clear days, climbers can look far below and see Seattle, Tacoma, and other cities where more than one million people live.

The First Woman Climber

Fay Fuller, a nineteen-year-old school teacher, was the first woman to climb Mount Rainier. During the summer of 1890, she reached the top along with four men.

Fay wore boy's boots, a flannel suit, and a long coat. She carried dried beef, boiled eggs, and canned sardines in her pockets.

Fay later wrote that steam vents at the top looked "like a row of tea kettles," and "the gentlemen's moustaches were frozen like ice."

Visiting the Park

You don't have to be a mountain climber to enjoy Mount Rainier National Park. You and your family can drive through the park and up the mountain's slopes to visitor centers. The park's highest visitor center is at Sunrise, elevation 6,400 feet (1,950 m).

Highways in the park offer beautiful views of Mt. Rainier.

Another visitor center is at Paradise, elevation 5,400 feet (1,647 m). Paradise Inn, a large hotel, is also at Paradise. It was built in 1917. The road to Paradise is the only park road kept open in the winter.

The Henry M. Jackson Visitor Center is located at Paradise.

At these visitor centers (and the visitor center at Longmire), you can get trail maps. The park has 300 miles (485 km) of trails. Some trails are short, so you can easily enjoy a closer view of the park's plants and animals.

Park Trails

The forest grows on the lower portion of Mount Rainier's slopes. In the lowest part of the forest, more rain than snow falls in the winter. The trails wind beneath tall western hemlocks, Douglas firs, and western red cedars. Some of these trees have grown to

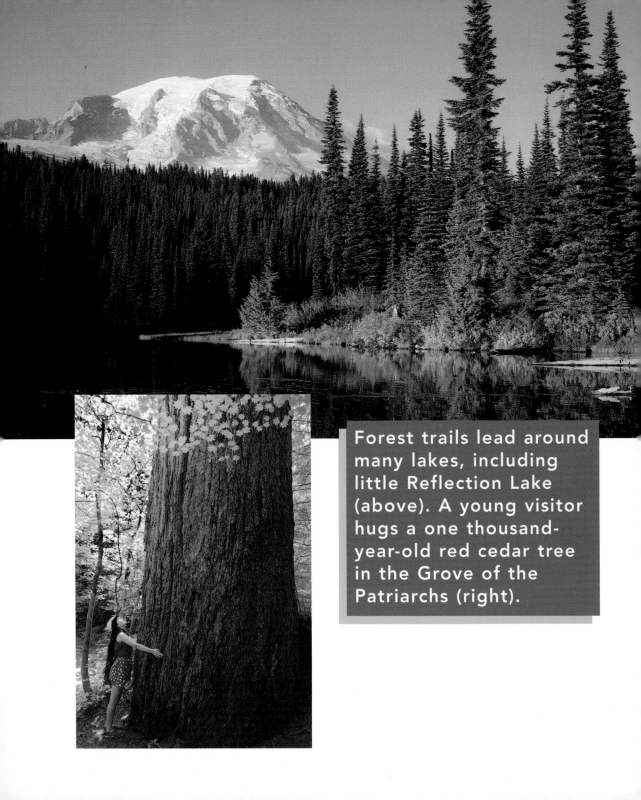

Forest trails lead around many lakes, including little Reflection Lake (above). A young visitor hugs a one thousand-year-old red cedar tree in the Grove of the Patriarchs (right).

a giant size. A short trail takes you to the Grove of the Patriarchs. The grove is located on an island in the Ohanapecosh (Oh-hannah-puh-kosh) River. These trees are more than 200 feet (61 m) tall and are almost one thousand years old!

In the higher part of the forest, winter storms bring more snow than rain. Trails lead past lakes and beneath silver firs, mountain hemlocks, and

Among the many kinds of animals and birds in the forest are black-tail deer, red-tailed hawks, and Douglas' squirrels.

Alaska yellow cedars. As you hike the forest trails you may see deer, squirrels, porcu-pines, red-tailed hawks, and woodpeckers.

Listen for a loud "eeenk" near rocks in the higher part of the forest. This sound comes from a pika, a guinea-piglike animal. Pikas collect grass and stack it in the sun to dry. Then they store their "hay" under rocks to eat in the winter.

A pika takes a break from gathering food for the winter to munch on a flower.

If you stop for a lunchtime picnic, you are sure to see gray jays. Hikers call these birds "camp robbers." The jays perch on trees near picnickers looking for bread crumbs or crackers.

In early fall, you may see black bears feasting on the juicy berries of huckleberry bushes. The bears grow fat on the berries, then take their long winter's sleep in the forest.

Higher up the mountain are meadows. Deep snow covers

Gray jays (above) enjoy sharing a hiker's lunch. Visitors should stay a safe distance away from the park's black bears (right).

the meadow trails during the winter. But by early July, the snow has melted, and wildflowers bloom. There are forty kinds of flowers that burst into color along meadow trails.

Visitors come from all over the world to see the wildflowers (above). Trees grow in clumps in the park's meadows (left).

Some of them are: blue lupine, yellow glacier lilies, and red Indian paintbrush.

Trees such as mountain hemlock, Alaska yellow cedar, and subalpine fir grow alone or in clumps in the meadows. Summers here are short, so the trees grow very slowly. Most of the trees are small, but some are 250 years old!

You may see deer, bear, and elk. When the snow melts, these animals move from the forests to the meadows to look for food.

The white-tailed ptarmigan (TAR-ma-gan) looks like a chicken. It lives in the meadows year round. In the summer, its

The white-tailed ptarmigan's summer (left) and winter (right) feathers help it to hide from its enemies.

feathers are spotted brown. For winter, it grows white feathers. It even grows feathers on its feet for easy walking in the snow.

Above the meadows, trails cross rocks, snowfields, and glaciers. Winters are harsh. Sometimes it even snows in

Hikers rest from the icy trails and enjoy the view of one of the park's many glaciers.

the summer. There are no trees this high up. Small plants such as heather grow next to rocks. The rocks shelter the heather from strong winds. It takes ten years for this heather to grow just one-quarter of an inch (.63 centimeters).

At the highest part of the mountain, only snow algae and map lichens grow. Snow algae are tiny plants that grow in snow. They color the snow pink. Map lichens are a kind of plant that grows on flat rocks. Tiny deer mice live year round among the rocks and snow. They eat bugs and spiders blown onto the mountain by the wind. They even search for snacks in climbers' packs! In summertime, mountain

At high elevations, snow algae turns the snow pink (above). Ask a park ranger where you can hike to see a glacier up close (right).

goats may be seen near these trails.

Many icy trails are steep and sometimes dangerous. Ask park rangers about a safe place to hike to see the glaciers.

The Mountain is Out!

Mount Rainier is so high that it is often hidden in the clouds. So, hope for a clear day when you visit the park. That is the kind of day when the mountain's icy top can be seen from far away. On these days, people near and far smile and say, "The mountain is out!"

In clear weather, people from miles away can enjoy seeing Mount Rainier.

To Find Out More

Here are some additional resources to help you learn more about Mount Rainier National Park, Washington State, volcanoes, and more:

 Books

Davis, Wendy. **Douglas Fir.** Children's Press, 1997.

Dobson, Steven. **John Muir: Man of the Wild Places.** Children's Press, 1991.

Fradin, Dennis B. **Washington.** Children's Press, 1994.

George, Michael. **Glaciers.** Creative Editions, 1992.

Lye, Keith. **Mountains.** Raintree Steck-Vaughn, 1996.

Taylor, Barbara. **Forest Life.** Dorling Kindersley, 1993.

Taylor, Barbara. **Meadow.** Dorling Kindersley, 1992.

Walker, Sally. **Volcanoes: Earth's Inner Fire.** Lerner, 1994.

Organizations and Online Sites

Mount Rainier
*http://www.inch.com/
~dipper/wa.html*

Here you'll find a clickable map and dozens of links to Mt. Rainier-related sites.

Mount Rainier
National Park
*http://portoftacoma.com/
tacoma/county/
mtrainierpark.html*

This site contains the history of the park, statistics, and plenty of other information.

Mount Rainier National
Park Associates
9230 41st Avenue NE
Seattle, WA 98115

National Parks and
Conservation Association
1776 Massachusetts
  Avenue, NW
Washington, DC 20036

National Park Service
Pacific West Area
600 Harrison Street
Suite 600
San Francisco, CA 94101
http://www.nps.gov/

Online Highways—Travel
Guide to Washington
*http://www.ohwy.com/wa/
homepage.htm*

Tons of information on Washington travel, history, culture, and outdoor adventure. Also, links to Idaho, Oregon, and British Columbia Online Highways.

Important Words

century period of one hundred years

climate the usual weather in a certain place

elevation height above the level of the sea

ice ax tool shaped like the letter T, with a sharp point at the bottom and a metal head for chipping ice at the top

naturalist person who studies animals and plants

national park large section of land set aside by the government for public enjoyment

Index

Meet the Authors

Sharlene and Ted Nelson have lived near Mount Rainier National Park for many years. They have hiked the mountain's trails with their children and grandchildren.

The Nelsons have written many articles and books about West Coast lighthouses, the Columbia River, and various children's topics. Other True Books they have written for Children's Press include *Hawaii Volcanoes National Park, Mount St. Helens National Volcanic Monument,* and *Olympic National Park.*